The Bow in the Cloud

The Bow in the Cloud
John R. MacDuff

Edited and Mildly Modernized by
Ralph I. Tilley

LITS Books
PO Box 405
Sellersburg, Indiana 47172

The Bow in the Cloud
John R. MacDuff
Introduction by Ralph I. Tilley
Revised edition
Copyright © 2014 Ralph I. Tilley

*All hymns and poetry quoted in this book are in
the public domain, to the best of the editor's knowledge.*

ISBN - 10: 0990395006
ISBN - 13: 978-0-9903950-0-3

LITS Books
PO Box 405
Sellersburg, Indiana 47172

*Ralph I. Tilley is the executive director of Life in the Spirit
Ministries and online editor of Life in the Spirit Journal.
For further information, contact litsjournal.org.*

Books available at either . . . litsjournal.org or amazon.com

*LITS Books is a division of Life in the Spirit Ministries,
a not-for-profit corporation. While funds are necessary
to operate this ministry, our mission is ministry—not money.*

This volume is affectionately dedicated
to all of God's people,
who at this time are walking the path of suffering.

Acknowledgement
This book was originally published by
Robert Carter and Brothers, New York, 1870.

Contents

Introduction

by Ralph I. Tilley

All people experience some degree of suffering, at one time or another, during their earthly sojourn. There are the usual physical ailments, illnesses, and injuries that are common to all people in all places in all times. Then there is the wide assortment of emotional and psychological pain, which can be summed up in one word—*loss*.

These *losses* can be some of the most difficult for any of us to undergo and walk through: the loss of employment; the loss of a friendship; the loss of a position; the loss of wealth; the loss of a child, a sibling, a parent, a spouse, etc. John R. Macduff points the Christian to the sovereign God, who desires to use our trials to bring glory to himself, to deepen our faith, and to produce a greater maturity in our understanding and walk of faith. He demonstrates godly wisdom as he comes alongside the suffering believer, pointing him and her always to the unchanging and compassionate Father of mercies.

Macduff was clear about who his target audience was in writing these thirsty-one devotionals: "This little book is intended to be seen by no eyes but weeping ones. It addresses no hearts but broken ones. It is to speak of sorrows with which a stranger cannot inter-meddle."

This Scottish pastor and author was passionate when he wrote about this subject of suffering. Many of his original sentences were written with exclamation points, in the upper case, and italicized. He believed in the promises of God and the power of the Holy Spirit to bring encouragement to each sufferer. He wrote as a warmhearted, knowledgeable and empathizing pastor. He was convinced that God could use the "cloud," as well as the "bow" to fulfill his purposes.

About the author. John Ross MacDuff (1818-1895) was born May 23, 1818, at Bonhard, near Perth, Scotland. After studying at the University of Edinburgh, he became in 1842 parish minister of Kettins, Forfarshire; in 1849 of St. Madoes, Perthshire; and in 1855 of Sandyford, Glasgow. He received the Doctor of Divinity degree from the University of Glasgow in 1862, and about the same time also from the University of New York. He retired from pastoral work in 1871, and thereafter lived at Chislehurst, Kent, for the purpose of focusing entirely on writing. MacDuff was a prolific author of devotional works, as well as a composer of hymns. Several of his writings are still in circulation.

There are several editions of this book on the Internet in the form of e-books. However, since I first came across this devotional by MacDuff, I became increasingly convinced that it deserved to be reprinted, although I felt the language needed to be edited and mildly modernized. This I have done.

In addition to updating the language of the book, I have also included Bible references, which MacDuff rarely included (I suspect this was because he knew his audience was steeped in the Scriptures, unlike those in our day). Furthermore, as was consistent with the times, MacDuff used the Authorized Version of the Bible (King James Version) in his writings, which I have also modernized. The reader must be advised that in MacDuff's quotations of Scripture, he quite often is imprecise: sometimes rephrasing the word order, sometimes changing verb tenses. Additionally, I have inserted the birth and death dates of those authors MacDuff quotes, as well as adding a selection from a classic hymn at the conclusion of each devotional.

After first reading this excellent devotional, I said to myself that all suffering Christians could be greatly ministered to by the Lord through this godly man's insights. That is why I have edited and reprinted this work—so that some suffering saint may take encouragement from the Lord by way of this instrument of grace and mercy.

In the words of the apostle, "Blessed be the God and Father of our Lord Jesus Christ, the Father of mercies and God of all comfort, who comforts us in all our affliction . . ." (2 Cor. 1:3-4 ESV).

Ralph I. Tilley, Editor
Soli Deo Gloria

- *Day 1* -

Sovereignty

"The Lord reigns."
Psalm 93:1

No *bow of promise* in the dark and cloudy day shines more radiant-ly than this: God, my God, the God who gave Jesus—orders all events and overrules all for my good!

"When I" says He, "bring a cloud over the earth" (Gen. 9:14), He has no wish to conceal the hand which shadows for a time earth's brightest prospects. It is He alike who "brings" the cloud, who brings us into it, and in mercy leads us through it! His kingdom rules over all. "The lot is cast into the lap, but the whole disposing thereof is of the LORD" (Prov. 16:33). We are tenants at will; but, blessed thought, at God's will. He puts the burden on, and keeps it on, and at His own time will remove it!

Beware of brooding over second causes. It is the worst form of atheism! When our most fondly cherished gourds (see Jonah 4:7) are smitten—our fairest flowers lie withered in our bosom—this is the silencer of all reflections, "But GOD prepared the worm" (Jonah 4:7). When the temple of the soul is smitten with lightning—its pillars rent—"The Lord is in His holy temple" (Hab. 2:20). Accident, chance, fate, destiny, have no place in the Christian's creed. His is no unpiloted vessel left to the mercy of the storm—no weed left to the sport of the fitful waves. "The voice of the Lord is upon the waters" (Ps. 29:3). There is but one explanation of all that befalls him: "I will be silent, I opened not my mouth; because You did it" (Ps. 39:9).

Death seems to the human spectator the most capricious and wayward of events. But not God. The keys of Hades are in the hands of this same reigning God! Look at the parable of the fig tree. Its prolonged existence, or its doom as a cumberer, forms matter of conversation in Heaven; the axe cannot be laid at its root until God gives the warrant! How much more will this be the case regarding every "tree of righteousness, the planting of the Lord" (Isa. 61:3)? It will be watched over by Him, "lest any one should hurt it" (Isa. 27:3). Every trembling fiber He will care for; and if it is made early to succumb to the inevitable stroke, "who knows not in all these, that the hand of the Lord has wrought this?" (Job 12:9).

Be it mine to merge my own will into Him—not to cavil at His ways, or seek to have one jot or tittle of that will altered; but to lie passively in His hands; to take the bitter as well as the sweet, knowing that the cup is mingled by One who loves me too well to add one ingredient that might have been spared!

Who can wonder that the sweet psalmist of Israel should seek, as he sees it spanning the lowering heavens, to fix the arrested gaze of a whole world on the softened tints of this Bow of Comfort—"The

Sovereignty

Lord reigns; let the earth rejoice" (Ps. 97:1).

"And it shall come to pass,
when I bring a cloud over the earth,
that the bow shall be seen in the cloud."

There's not a plant or flower below,
but makes Thy glories known,
And clouds arise, and tempests blow,
by order from Thy throne;
While all that borrows life from Thee
is ever in Thy care;
And everywhere that we can be,
Thou, God art present there.

(Taken from *I Sing the Mighty Power of God* by Isaac Watts, 1674-1748)

- *Day 2* -

A Loving Purpose

*"Let the LORD be magnified, which has
pleasure in the prosperity of his servant."*
Psalm 35:27

What is prosperity? Is it the threads of life weaved into a bright tissue? Is it a full cup of ample riches, worldly applause, an un- broken circle? No, these are often a snare—received without gratitude—dimming the soul to its nobler destinies. Often spiritually, it rather means God taking us by the hand into the lowly valleys of *humiliation*; leading us as He did his servant Job of old, out of his sheep, oxen, camels, health, wealth, children, in order that we may be brought to lie before Him in the dust, and say, "Blessed be the name of the LORD" (Job 1:21).

Yes, the very reverse of what is known in the world as prosperity (generally) forms the background on which the Bow of Promise is seen. God smiles on us through these raindrops and teardrops of sorrows! He loves us too well. He has too great an interest in our spiritual welfare to permit us to live on in what is misnamed *prosperity*. When He sees duties languidly performed, or coldly neglected—the heart deadened, and love to Himself congealed by the absorbing power of a present world, He puts a thorn in our nest to drive us to the wing, and prevent our being a groveler forever!

I may not be able now to understand the mystery of these dealings. I may be asking through tears, "Why this unkind arrest on my earthly happiness? "Why so premature a lopping of my boughs of promise? Such a speedy withering of my most cherished gourd" (see Jonah 4:7)? The answer is plain: it is your soul prosperity He has in view.

Believe it, your truest Ebenezers (see 1 Sam. 7:12) will yet be raised close by your Zarephaths (the place of furnaces; see 1 Kings 17:8f). His afflictions are no arbitrary appointments. There is a righteous necessity in all He does. As He lays His chastening hand upon you, and leads you by ways you know not, and which you never would have chosen, He whispers the gentle accents in your ear, "Beloved I wish above all things that you would prosper and be in health, even as your soul prospers" (3 John 1:2).

Best in the quiet consciousness that all is well. Murmur at nothing which brings you nearer to His own loving Presence. Be thankful for your very cares, because you can confidingly cast them all upon Him. He has your temporal and eternal prosperity too much at heart to appoint one superfluous pang, one redundant stroke. Commit, therefore, all that concerns yourself to His keeping and leave it there!

"And it shall come to pass,
when I bring a cloud over the earth,

that the bow shall be seen in the cloud."

Sometime, when all life's lessons have been learned,
And sun and stars forevermore have set,
The things which our weak judgments here have spurned,
The things o'er which we grieved with lashes wet,
Will flash before us out of life's dark night,
As stars shine most in deeper tints of blue;
And we shall see how all God's plans are right,
And how what seemed reproof was love most true.

And we shall see how, while we frown and sigh,
God's plans go on as best for you and me;
How, when we called, He heeded not our cry,
Because His wisdom to the end could see.
And e'en as prudent parents disallow
Too much of sweet to craving babyhood,
So God, perhaps, is keeping from us now
Life's sweetest things, because it seemeth good.

(Taken from *Sometime* by May Riley Smith, 1842-1927)

- *Day 3* -

The Safe Retreat

"A man shall be as an hiding place from the wind, and covert from
the tempest; as rivers of water in a dry place,
as the shadow of a great rock in a weary land."
Isaiah 32:2

"A man"—this first word forms the key to this precious verse: it is
the Man, Christ Jesus!

And when and where is He thus revealed to His people as their hiding place? It is, as with Elijah of old, in the whirlwind and the
storm! Amid the world's bright sunshine, in the calm of tranquil
skies—uninterrupted prosperity—they seek Him not! But when the
clouds begin to gather, and the sun is swept from their firmament,
when they have learned the insecurity of all earthly refuges, then
the prayer ascends, "My heart is overwhelmed, lead me to the Rock
that is higher than I" (Ps. 61:2). The earthquake, the tempest, the
fire, and then "the still small voice" (1 Kings 19:12)!

Sorrowing believer, you have indeed a Sure Covert—a Strong Tower which cannot be shaken! The world has its coverts too. But they

cannot stand the day of trial. The wind passes over them and they are gone! But the louder the hurricane, the more will it endear to you the abiding Shelter; the deeper in the clefts of this Rock, the safer you are.

A Man! Delight often to dwell on the humanity of Jesus—you have a Brother on the throne, a living Kinsman—One who "knows your frame" (Ps. 103:14) and who, by the exquisite sympathies of His exalted human nature, can gauge, as none other can, the depths of your sorrow.

An earthly friend comes to you in trial; he has never known bereavement, and therefore cannot enter into your woe. Another comes: he has been again and again in the furnace; his heart has been touched tenderly as your own; he can feelingly sympathize with you. It is so with Jesus. As Man, He has passed through every experience of suffering. He has Himself known the storm from which He offers you shelter. He is the Rock, yet a Man! "Mighty to save," (Isa. 63:1) yet mighty in compassion! "Immanuel, God with us" (Isa. 7:14)! He is like the bow in the material heavens, which, while its summit is in the clouds, either base of its arc rests on earth; or like the oak, which, while it can wrestle with the tempest, yet invites the feeblest bird to fold its wing on its branches!

Mourner, go sit under your "Beloved's shadow with great delight" (Song 2:3). Hide in His wounded side! The hand which pierced you is ordering your trials. He who roused the storm is the hiding place from it, and as you journey on—gloomy clouds mustering around you—let this bright Bow of Comfort ever arrest your drooping eye, "Wherefore in all things it was necessary to be made like unto His brothers. . . . For in that He Himself has suffered, being tempted, He is able to encourage them that are tempted" (Heb. 2:17-18).

> "And it shall come to pass,
> when I bring a cloud over the earth,
> that the bow shall be seen in the cloud."

O safe to the Rock that is higher than I,
My soul in its conflicts and sorrows would fly;
So sinful, so weary, Thine, Thine, would I be;
Thou blest "Rock of Ages," I'm hiding in Thee.

. . .

How oft in the conflict, when pressed by the foe,
I have fled to my refuge and breathed out my woe;
How often, when trials like sea billows roll,
Have I hidden in Thee, O Thou Rock of my soul.

(Taken from *Hiding in Thee* by William O. Cushing, 1823-1902)

- *Day 4* -

The Reason for Chastisement

"Whom the Lord loves he chastens."
Hebrews 12:6

What?! God loves me when He is discharging His quiver upon me, emptying me from vessel to vessel, causing the sun of my earthly joys to set in clouds? Yes! O afflicted, tossed with tempest; He chastens you because He loves you! This trial comes from His own tender, loving hand—His own tender, unchanging heart!

Are you laid on a sickbed? Are sorrowful months and wearisome nights appointed unto you? Let this be the pillow on which your aching head reclines—it is *because* He loves me!

Is it bereavement that has swept your heart and desolated your dwelling? He appointed that chamber of death; He opened that tomb, *because* he loves you! As it is the suffering child of the family which claims a mother's deepest affections and most tender solicitude, so have you at this moment embarked on your side the most tender love and solicitude of a chastening heavenly Father. He loved you into this sorrow, and He will love you through it. There is

- 10 -

nothing capricious in His dealings. Love is the reason of all He does. There is no drop of wrath in that cup you are called upon to drink. "I do believe," says Lady Powerscourt (1800-1836), "He has purchased these afflictions for us as well as every thing else. Blessed be His name, it is a part of His covenant to visit us with the rod." What says our adorable Lord Himself? The words were spoken, not when He was on earth, a sojourner in a sorrowing world, but when enthroned amid the glories of Heaven "As many as I love, I rebuke and chasten" (Rev. 3:19).

Believer, rejoice in the thought that the rod, the chastening rod, is in the hands of the living, loving Savior, who died for you! Tribulation is the King's highway, and yet that highway is paved with love. As some flowers before shedding their fragrance require to be pressed, so does your God find it necessary to bruise you. As some birds are said to sing their sweetest notes when the thorn pierces their bosom, so does He appoint affliction to lacerate, that you may be driven to the wing, singing, in your upward soaring, "My heart is fixed, O God, my heart is fixed" (Ps. 57:7)! "Those," says the heavenly Robert Leighton (1611-1684), "He means to make the most resplendent, He hath oftenest His tools upon." "Our troubles," says another, "seem in His Word to be ever in His mind. Perhaps half the commands and half the promises He gives us there, are given us as troubled men."

Be it ours to say, "Lord, I will love you, not only despite your rod, but because of your rod." I will rush into the very arms that are chastising me! When your voice calls, as to Abraham of old, to prepare for bitter trial, be it mine to respond with bounding heart, "Here am I"—and to read in the Bow which spans my darkest cloud, "He chastens because He loves!"

> "And it shall come to pass,
> when I bring a cloud over the earth,
> that the bow shall be seen in the cloud."

If we could know beyond today
* As God doth know,*
Why dearest treasures pass away,
And tears must flow;
* And why the darkness leads to light,*
Why dreary days will soon grow bright,
* Some day life's wrong will be made right,*
Faith tells us so.

(Taken from *If we Could See Beyond Today*
by Norman J. Clayton, 1903-1992)

- Day 5 -

Immutability

The unchangeableness of God! What an anchor for the storm-tossed! Change is our portion here. Scenes are altering. Joys are fading. Friends, some of them, are removed to a distance— others have gone to the longest home of all! Who, amid these checkered experiences does not sigh for something permanent, stable, enduring? The vessel has again and again slipped its earthly moorings. We long for some secure and sheltered harbor.

"I change not!" Heart and flesh may faint—yes, do faint and fail—but there is an unfainting, unfailing, unvarying God. All the changes in the world around cannot affect Him. Our own fitfulness cannot alter Him. When we are depressed, downcast, fluctuating, our treacherous hearts turning aside like a broken bow—He is without one "shadow of turning" (James 1:17). "God who cannot lie" (Titus 1:2), is the superscription on His eternal throne, and inscribed on all his dealings.

"I change not!" For whom does He span the darkened sky with this Bow of comfort? It is for the sons of Jacob, His own covenant people. Those clothed like Jacob of old, in the garment of the true "Elder Brother," through whom they have obtained their spiritual inheritance.

Precious name! It forms a blessed guarantee that nothing can befall me but what is for my good. I cannot doubt His faithfulness. I dare not arraign the rectitude of His dispensations. It is covenant love which is now darkening my earthly horizon. This hour He is the same as when He "spared not His own Son" (Rom. 8:32)! Oh, instead of wondering at my trials, let me rather wonder that He has borne with me so long. It is of the Lord's unchanging mercies that I am not consumed. Had He been man, changeable, vacillating, as myself, long before now would He have spurned me away, and consigned me to the doom of the cumberer. But, "My thoughts are not your thoughts, neither are your ways my ways, says the Lord" (Isa. 55:8). He is without any variableness. Yes, in this dark and cloudy day I will lift up my eyes to the covenant token, and sing through my tears, "Happy is he who has the God of Jacob for his help—whose hope is in the Lord his God" (Ps. 146:5)!

"And it shall come to pass,
when I bring a cloud over the earth,
that the bow shall be seen in the cloud."

Change is our portion here:
soon fades the summer sky;
The landscape droops in autumn sear,
and spring-flowers bloom to die;

Immutability

But faithful is Jehovah's word,
  "I will be with thee," saith the Lord.

Change is our portion here:
  along the heavenly road,
In faith and hope and holy fear,
  in love towards our God.
How often we distrust the word,
  "I will be with thee," saith the Lord.

Change is our portion here:
  yet midst our changing lot,
Midst withering flowers and tempests drear,
  there is that changes not.
Unchangeable Jehovah's word,
  "I will be with thee," saith the Lord.

Changeless, the way of peace:
  changeless, Emmanuel's name;
Changeless, the covenant of grace;
  eternally the same.
"I change not," is a Father's word.
  "And I am with thee," saith the Lord.

(*Change is Our Portion Here* by James H. Evans, 1785-1849)

- *Day 6* -

Divine Sympathy

"I know their sorrows."
Exodus 3:7

Man cannot say so. There are many sensitive fibers in the soul that the best and most tender human sympathy cannot touch. But the Prince of Sufferers, He who led the way in the path of sorrow, "knows our frame" (Ps. 103:14).

When crushing bereavement lies like ice on the heart; when the dearest earthly friend cannot enter into the peculiarities of our grief, Jesus can, Jesus does! He who once bore my sins also carried my sorrows. That eye, now on the throne, was once dim with weeping! I can think in all my afflictions, "He was afflicted" (Isa. 53:7); in all my tears, "Jesus wept" (John 11:35).

Israel had long groaned under bondage. God appeared not to *know* it. He seemed, like Baal, "asleep" (see 1 Kings 18:27); yet at that very moment was His pitying eye wistfully beholding His enslaved people. It was then He said, "I know their sorrows."

He may *seem* at times thus to forget and forsake us—leaving us to utter the plaintive cry, "Has God forgotten to be gracious?" (Ps. 77:9), when all the while He is bending over us in the most tender love. He often suffers our needs to attain their extremity—that He may stretch forth His compassionate hand, and reveal the plenitude of His Grace! "You have seen the end *intended* by the Lord—that the Lord is very compassionate and merciful" (James 5:11).

And *knowing* our sorrows is a blessed guarantee that none will be sent but what He sees to be needful. "I will not," says He, "make a full end of you, but I will correct you in measure" (Jer. 30:11.) All He sends is precisely meted out—wisely apportioned. There is nothing accidental or fortuitous—no redundant thorn, no superfluous pang. He "puts our tears into His bottle" (Ps. 56:8). Each one is *counted*—drop by drop, tear by tear, they are sacred things among the treasures of God!

Suffering believer, the iron may have entered deeply into your soul, yet rejoice! Great is your honor—"you are partaker with Christ in His sufferings" (1 Pet. 4:13). Look upward to this bright Bow encircling your dark sky! Jesus, a sorrowing, sympathizing Jesus, *knows* your aching pangs and burning tears, and He will "come down to deliver you" (Ex. 3:8)!

> "And it shall come to pass,
> when I bring a cloud over the earth,
> that the bow shall be seen in the cloud."

Under His wings, what a refuge in sorrow!
How the heart yearningly turns to His rest!

Often when earth has no balm for my healing,
There I find comfort and there I am blest.

Under His wings, O what precious enjoyment!
There will I hide till life's trials are o'er;
Sheltered, protected, no evil can harm me,
Resting in Jesus I'm safe evermore.

(Taken from *Under His Wings* by William O. Cushing, 1823-1902)

- *Day 7* -

A Gracious Condition

"If need be."
1 Peter 1:6

What a blessed motto and superscription over the dark lintels of sorrow—"if need be!" Every arrow from the quiver of God is feathered with it! Write it, child of affliction, over every trial your God sees necessary to send! If he calls you down from the sunny mountain heights to the dark glades, hear Him saying, "There is a need be." If he has dashed the cup of earthly prosperity from your lips, curtailed your creature comforts, diminished your "basket and your kneading bowl" (Deut. 28:5), hear Him saying, "There is a need be." If He has ploughed and furrowed your soul with severe bereavement, extinguished light after light in your dwelling, hear Him thus stilling the tumult of your grief—"There is a need be."

Yes! believe it, there is some profound reason for your trial, which at present may be undiscernible. No furnace will be hotter than that He sees to be needed. Sometimes, indeed, His teachings are mysterious. We can with difficulty spell out the letters, *God is love!* We can see no bright light, no luminous Bow in *our* cloud. It is all mystery; not one break is there in the sky! No! Hear what God the Lord does speak: "If need be." He does not long leave His people alone, if He sees the chariot wheels dragging heavily, He will take His own means to sever them from an absorbing love of the world—to pursue them out of self—and dislodge usurping clay idols that may have vaulted on the throne which He alone may occupy. Before your present trial He may have seen your love waxing cold, your influence for good lessening. As the sun puts out the fire, the sun of earthly prosperity may have been extinguishing the fires of your soul; you may have been shining less brightly for Christ—effecting some guilty compromise with an insinuating and seductive world. He has appointed the very discipline and dealing necessary—nothing else—nothing less could have done!

Be still, and know that He is God! That "need be," remember, is in the hands of Infinite Love, Infinite Wisdom, Infinite Power. Trust Him in little things as well as in great things—in trifles as well as in emergencies. Seek to have an unquestioning faith. Though other paths, doubtless, would have been selected by you had the choice been in your hands, but listen to His voice at every turn of the road, saying, "THIS is the way, walk you in it" (Isa. 30:21).

We may not be able to understand it now, but one day we shall come to find, that *affliction* is one of God's most blessed angels, a ministering spirit, "sent forth to minister to them who are heirs of salvation" (Heb. 1:14). There would be no Bow in the material Heaven but for the Cloud! Lovelier, indeed, to the eye, is the azure blue, the fleecy summer vapor, or the gold and vermillion of western sunsets. But what would become of the earth if no dark clouds from time to time hung over it, distilling their treasures, reviving and refreshing its drooping vegetable tribes? Is it otherwise with the soul? No. The *cloud of sorrow* is needed; its every raindrop has an inner meaning of love! If, even now, afflicted one, these clouds are gathering, and the tempest sighing, lift up your eye to the divine scroll gleaming in the darkened heavens, and remember that He who has put the Bow of Promise there, saw also a "need be" for the cloud on which it rests!

> "And it shall come to pass,
> when I bring a cloud over the earth,
> that the bow shall be seen in the cloud."

Be still, my soul: the Lord is on thy side.
Bear patiently the cross of grief or pain.
Leave to thy God to order and provide;
In every change, He faithful will remain.

. . .

Thy hope, thy confidence let nothing shake;
All now mysterious shall be bright at last.
Be still, my soul: the waves and winds still know
His voice Who ruled them while He dwelt below.

(Taken from *Be Still My Soul* by Katharina von Schlegel, 1697-1768)

- Day 8 -

Presence and Rest

"My presence shall go with you, and I will give you rest."
Exodus 33:14

Moses asked to be shown "the way" (Ex. 33:13). Here is the answer: the "way" is not shown, but better than this, God says, "Trust Me, I will go with you!"

Afflicted one, I hear the voice addressing you from the cloudy pillar. It is a wilderness promise which "the God of Jeshurun" (Deut. 33:26) speaks to his spiritual Israel still. He who led his people of old "like a flock by the hand of Moses and Aaron" (Ps. 77:20), will manifest toward you the same Shepherd-love. The way may be very different from what we could have wished, what we would have chosen. But the choice is in better hands. He has his own wise and righteous ends in every devious turning in it.

Who can look back on the past leadings of God without gratitude and thankfulness? When His sheep have been conducted to the rougher parts of the wilderness, He, their Shepherd, has "gone before them" (John 10:4). When their fleeces were torn, and they were foot-sore and weary, He has borne them in His arms. His presence has lightened every cross and sweetened every care.

Let us trust Him for an unknown and checkered future. Other companionships we cherished may have failed us, but One who is better than the best, goes before us in His gracious Pillar-cloud. With Him for our portion, take what He will away, we must be happy; we can rise above the loss of the earthly gift, in the consciousness of the nobler possession and heritage we enjoy in the Great Bestower. He may have seen it necessary to level clay idols, that He, the All-Satisfying, might reign paramount and supreme. He may have seen it necessary to take earthly *presences* away in order to give us more of His own, and to lead us to breathe more earnestly the prayer, "If your presence goes not with us, carry us not hence" (Ex. 33:14).

He will not allow us to rear tabernacles on earth, and to write upon them, "This is my rest." No! Tenting time here—resting time yonder! But, "fear not," He seems to say, "you are not left unbefriended or unsolaced on the way, pilgrim in a pilgrim land! My presence shall go with you. In all your dark and cloudy days—in your hours of faintness and depression, in sadness and in sorrow, in loneliness and solitude, in life and in death! And when the journey is ended, the Pillar will be needed no more, I will give you rest." The earnest of Grace will be followed with the fruition of glory!

> "And it shall come to pass,
> when I bring a cloud over the earth,
> that the bow shall be seen in the cloud."

Lo, God is here! let us adore,
And own how dreadful is this place!
Let all within us feel His power,
And silent bow before His face.

Lo, God is here! Whom day and night
United choirs of angels sing;
To Him, enthroned above all height,
The hosts of Heaven their praises bring.

(Taken from *Lo, God is Here* by Gerhard Tersteegen, 1697-1769)

- *Day 9* -

The Giver and Taker

"The LORD gave, and the LORD has taken away;
blessed be the name of the LORD."
Job 1:21

Noble posture is this: to kneel and to adore! To see no hand but One! Sabeans, fire, whirlwind, sword—are all overlooked. The patriarch recognizes alone "the LORD" who gave and "the LORD" who had taken!

What is the cause of so much depression, overmuch sorrow, ungospel murmuring in our hours of trial? It is what Samuel Rutherford (1600-1661) calls, "Our looking to the confused rollings of the wheels of second causes"; a refusal to rise to "the height of the great argument" and confidingly to say, "The will of the Lord be done!"—a refusal to hear His voice—His own loving voice, mingling with the accents of the rudest storm—"It is I!"

"Shall there be disaster in a city, and the Lord has not done it" (Amos 3:6)? Is there a bitter drop in the cup, and the Lord has not mingled it? He loves His people too well to entrust their interests to any other. We are but clay in the hand of the Potter—vessels in the hand of the Refiner of silver. He metes out our portion. He appoints the bounds of our habitation. "The Lord God prepared the gourd"; "The Lord God prepared the worm" (Jonah 4:6-7). He is the Author alike of mercies and sorrows, of comforts and crosses. He breathes into our nostrils the breath of life; and it is at his summons the spirit returns "to the God who gave it" (Eccles. 12:7).

Oh, that we would seek ever to regard our own lives and the lives of those dear to us as a loan. God, as the Great Proprietor—who, when He sees it suitable, can revoke the grant or curtail the lease— "He gave!" All the mercies we have are lent mercies—by Him bestowed—by Him continued—by Him withheld.

And how often does He take away, that He may Himself enter the vacuum of the heart and fill it with His own ineffable presence and love! No loss can compensate for the absence of Him, but He can compensate for all losses.

Let us trust His love and faithfulness as a *taking* as well as a *giving* God. Often are sense and sight tempted to say, "Not so, Lord" (Acts 10:14). But Faith, resting on the promise, can exult in this Bow spanning the darkest cloud—"Even so, Father: for so it *seems* good in your sight" (Matt. 11:26).

> "And it shall come to pass,
> when I bring a cloud over the earth,
> that the bow shall be seen in the cloud."

Children of the heav'nly Father

The Giver and Taker

Safely in His bosom gather;
Nestling bird nor star in Heaven
Such a refuge e'er was given.

God His own doth tend and nourish;
In His holy courts they flourish;
From all evil things He spares them;
In His mighty arms He bears them.

Neither life nor death shall ever
From the Lord His children sever;
Unto them His grace He showeth,
And their sorrows all He knoweth.

Though He giveth or He taketh,
God His children ne'er forsaketh;
His the loving purpose solely
To preserve them pure and holy.

Lo, their very hairs He numbers,
And no daily care encumbers
Them that share His ev'ry blessing
And His help in woes distressing.

Praise the Lord in joyful numbers:
Your Protector never slumbers.
At the will of your Defender
Ev'ry foeman must surrender.

(*Children of the Heavenly Father*
by Karolina W. Sandall-Berg, 1832-1903)

- Day 10 -

Deliverance in Trouble

"Call upon me in the day of trouble:
I will deliver you, and you shall glorify me."
Psalm 50:15

How varied are our days of trouble—sickness, with its hours of restlessness and languor; bereavement, with its rifled treasures and aching hearts. Add to these: loss of substance—the curtailment or forfeiture of worldly possessions—riches taking to themselves wings and fleeing away; or, severer than all, the woundings of friends, abused confidence, withered affections, hopes scattered like the leaves of autumn!

But "God is our refuge and strength, a very present help in trouble" (Ps. 46:1). Tried one, He leaves not your defenseless head unsheltered in the storm—Call upon me!" He invites you into the pavilion of His own presence! Better the bitter Marah waters (see Ex. 15:22-24) with His healing, than the purest fountain of the world and no God! Better the hottest furnace flames with one there "like the Son of God" (Dan. 3:25), than that the dross should be suffered to accumulate, and the soul left to cleave to the dust! He, "the Purifier of silver" (Mal. 3:3), is seated by these flames tempering their fury. Yes, he gives the special promise, "I will deliver you." It may not be the deliverance we expect; the deliverance we have prayed for; the deliverance we could have wished. But shall not the sorest trial be well worth enduring, if this is the result of his chastening love—"You shall glorify me." Glorify Him! How? By a simple unreasoning faith—by meek, lowly, unmurmuring acquiescence in His dealings—these dealings endearing the Savior and His grace more than ever to our hearts.

The day of trouble led His saints in all ages thus to glorify Him. David never could have written his touching Psalms, nor Paul his precious Epistles, had not God cast them both into the crucible. To be the teachers of the Church of the future, they had to graduate in the school of affliction.

If He is appointing us similar discipline, let it be our endeavor to glorify Him by active obedience, as well as by passive resignation; not abandoning ourselves to selfish, moody, sentimental grief; but rather going forth on our great mission—our work and warfare— with a vaster estimate of the value of time and the grandeur of existence.

"Give glory to the Lord your God before He causes darkness; and before your feet stumble upon the dark mountains, and, while you look for light, He turns it into the shadow of death, and makes it gross darkness" (Jer. 13:16).

"And it shall come to pass,
when I bring a cloud over the earth,

that the bow shall be seen in the cloud."

In the hour of trial, Jesus, plead for me,
Lest by base denial I depart from Thee.
When Thou seest me waver, with a look recall,
Nor for fear or favor suffer me to fall.

With forbidden pleasures would this vain world charm,
Or its sordid treasures spread to work me harm,
Bring to my remembrance sad Gethsemane,
Or, in darker semblance, cross-crowned Calvary.

Should Thy mercy send me sorrow, toil and woe,
Or should pain attend me on my path below,
Grant that I may never fail Thy hand to see;
Grant that I may ever cast my care on Thee.

(Taken from *In the Hour of Trial* by James Montgomery, 1771-1854)

- *Day 11* -

Compassionate Love

*"Like as a father pities his children,
so the Lord pities them that fear him."*
Psalm 103:13

"Abba, Father" is a gospel word. A father bending over the sick bed of his weak or dying child; a mother pressing, in tender solicitude, an infant sufferer to her bosom. These are the earthly pictures of God. "Like as a father pities." "As one whom his mother comforts, so will I comfort you" (Isa. 66:13).

When tempted in our season of overwhelming sorrow to say, "Never has there been so dark a cloud, never a heart so stripped and desolate as mine," let this thought hush every murmur, "It is your Father's good pleasure" (Luke 12:32). The love and pity of the most tender earthly parent is but a dim shadow compared to the compassionate love of God. If your heavenly Father's smile has for the moment been exchanged for the chastening rod, be assured there is some deep necessity for the altered discipline. If there are unutterable yearnings in the soul of the earthly parent as the lancet is applied to the body of his child—infinitely more is it so with your covenant God as He subjects you to these deep woundings of heart! Finite wisdom has no place in His ordinations. An earthly father may err—is ever erring; but, "As for God His way is perfect" (Ps. 18:30). This is the explanation of His every dealing: "Your heavenly Father knows that you have need of all these things" (Matt. 6:32).

Trust Him when you cannot trace Him. Do not try to penetrate the cloud which He "brings over the earth," and to look through it. Keep your eye steadily fixed on the Bow. The mystery is God's, the promise is yours. Seek that the end of all His dispensations may be to make you more confiding. Without one misgiving commit your way to Him. He says regarding each child of His covenant family, what He said of Ephraim of old (and nevermore so than in a season of suffering), "I do earnestly remember him still" (Jer. 31:20). While now bending your head like a bulrush—your heart breaking with sorrow—remember His compassionate eye is upon you. Be it yours, even through blinding tears, to say, "Even so, Father."

> "And it shall come to pass,
> when I bring a cloud over the earth,
> that the bow shall be seen in the cloud."

All as God wills, who wisely heeds
To give or to withhold,
And knoweth more of all my needs,
Than all my prayers have told.

Enough that blessings undeserved
Have marked my erring track;

Compassionate Love

That, wheresoe'er my feet have swerved,
His chastening turned me back.

That more and more a providence
Of love is understood,
Making the springs of time and sense
Sweet with eternal good.

That death seems but a covered way
Which opens into light,
Wherein no blinded child can stray
Beyond the Father's sight.

And so the shadows fall apart.
And so the west winds play;
And all the windows of my heart
I open to the day.

(Taken from *As God Wills* by John G., Whittier, 1807-1892)

- *Day 12* -

The Blessed Hope

*"Looking for that blessed hope, and the glorious appearing
of the great God and our Savior Jesus Christ."*
Titus 2:13

What a bright Bow for a storm-wreathed sky! Hope is a joyous emotion! Poetry sings of it; music warbles its lofty aspirations; but alas, how often does it weave fantastic visions—give birth to shadowy dreams, which appear, and then vanish! In the morning the flowers of life are flourishing and growing up; in the evening a mysterious blight comes—they lie withered garlands at our feet! The longing aspirations of a whole lifetime seem realized—one wave of calamity overtakes us, and washes all away !

But, there is one "Blessed Hope" beyond the possibility of blight or decay—the "hope of the glory of God" (Rom. 5:2); the hope that "makes not ashamed" (Rom. 5:5); "the glorious appearing of the Great God our Savior!"

If we long on earth for the return of an absent friend or brother, separated from us for a season, by intervening oceans or continents; if we count the weeks or months until we can welcome him back again to the parental home, how should the Christian long for the return of the Brother of brothers, the Friend of friends? "I will come again," is His own gracious promise, "to receive you unto myself" (John 14:3).

Oh happy day! when He shall be "glorified in His saints" (2 Thess. 1:10)—when His people will suffer no more, and sin no more. No more beds of sickness, or aching heads—or fevered brows. No more opened graves, or bitter tears—and, better than all—no more guilty estrangements and traitor unholy hearts! It will be the bridal day of the soul. The body slumbering in the dust will be reunited a glorified body to the redeemed spirit. The grave shall be forever spoiled—death swallowed up in eternal victory. "So shall we ever be with the Lord" (1 Thess. 4:17).

Reader, do you "love His appearing" (2 Tim. 4:8)? Are you in the eager expectant attitude of those who are "looking for and hasting unto the coming of the day of God" (2 Pet. 3:12)? "For yet a little while, and He that shall come, will come, and will not tarry" (Heb. 10:37). If you are a child of the covenant, having conscious filial nearness to the throne of grace, you need not dread the throne of glory! True, He is the "great God," but He is "our Savior." It is a "Kinsman Redeemer" who is ordained "to judge the world in righteousness" (Ps. 9:8).

Yes! turn your eye often toward this bright Bow spanning a glorious future, for remember, it is "unto them that *look* for Him, shall he appear the second time without sin unto salvation" (Heb. 9:28).

"And it shall come to pass,

when I bring a cloud over the earth,
that the bow shall be seen in the cloud."

O shout aloud the tidings,
Repeat the joyful strain;
Let all the waiting nations
This message hear again;
The spotless Lamb of glory,
Who once for man was slain,
Soon o'er all the earth shall reign.

Looking for that blessèd hope,
Looking for that blessèd hope;
We know the hour is nearing,
The hour of His appearing,
We're looking for that blessèd hope

(Taken from *Looking for That Blessèd Hope* by Thoro Harris, 1874-1955)

- *Day 13* -

A Gracious Removal

*"The righteous . . . are taken away . . . from the evil to come.
He shall enter into peace: they shall rest in their beds."*
Isaiah 57:1-2

How this thought reconciles earth's saddest separations! The early
(we are apt to think the *too* early) graves of our loved and lost, have
saved them much sorrow, much suffering, much sin! Who can tell
what may have been brooding in a dark horizon? The fairest vessel—the life freighted with greatest promise—might have made
shipwreck on this world's treacherous sea. My God knows what
was best. If He plucked His lily soon, it was to save it some rough
blast. If He early folded His lamb, it was to save it having its fleece
soiled with earthly corruption. If the port of glory was soon entered,
it was because He foresaw threatening tempests that screened from
our limited vision—"So He brought them to the haven where they
would be (Ps. 107:30).

Yes, the *quiet haven*! The storms of life are over! That shore is un-
disturbed by one murmuring wave. He shall "enter (he has entered)
into peace" the rest which remains. Did the ransomed dead, at the

hour of their departure, sink into blank oblivion—inherit everlasting silence, sad indeed would be the pang of separation. But, "Weep not, she is not dead, but sleeps" (Luke 8:52). Yea, weep not; she is not dead, but lives! At the very moment earth's tears are falling, the spirit is sunning in the realms of everlasting day, safely housed, safely *Home*! The body rests in its bed. The grave is its couch of repose! We bid it the long goodnight in the joyful expectancy of a glorious reunion at the waking time of immortality—that "morning without clouds" (2 Sam. 23:4), whose "sun shall no more go down" (Isa. 60:20)!

Child of sorrow, mourning over the withdrawal of some beloved object of earthly affection! Dry your tears. An early death has been an early crown! The tie sundered here links you to the throne of God. You have a brother, a sister, a child, in Heaven! You are the relative of a ransomed saint! We are proud when we hear of our friends being *advanced* in this world. What are the world's noblest promotions in comparison with that of the believer at death, when he graduates from grace to glory, when he exchanges the pilgrim warfare for the eternal rest?

Often, in your hours of sadness, contrast the certainty of present bliss, with the possibilities of a suffering, sorrowing, sinning future—the joys in possession, with the evils which might have been in reversion. You may now, like the Shunammite of old, be gazing with tearful eye on some withered blossom, but when the question is put, "Is it well with you? Is it well with your husband? Is it well with the child" (2 Kings 4:26)?—in the elevating confidence that they have "entered into peace" and are "resting in their beds," be it yours joyfully to answer, "It is well!"

A Gracious Removal

"And it shall come to pass,
when I bring a cloud over the earth,
that the bow shall be seen in the cloud."

When peace, like a river, attendeth my way,
When sorrows like sea billows roll;
Whatever my lot, Thou has taught me to say,
It is well, it is well, with my soul.

.   .   .

For me, be it Christ, be it Christ hence to live:
If Jordan above me shall roll,
No pang shall be mine, for in death as in life
Thou wilt whisper Thy peace to my soul.

(Taken from *It is Well With My Soul* by Horatio G. Spafford, 1828-1888)

- *Day 14* -

Unveiled Mysteries

"What I do you know not now; but you shall know hereafter."
John 13:7

Much is baffling and perplexing to us in God's present dealings. "What!" we are often ready to exclaim, "could not the cup have been less bitter, the trial less severe, the road less rough and dreary?" "Hush your misgivings," says a gracious God; "arraign not the rectitude of my dispensations. You shall yet see all revealed and made bright in the mirror of eternity!"

"What I do"—it is all my doing—my appointment. You have but a partial view of these dealings—they are seen by the eye of sense through a dim and distorted medium. You can see nothing but plans crossed, and gourds laid low (see Jonah 4:7), and "beautiful rods broken" (Ezek. 19:12). But I see the end from the beginning. "Shall not the Judge of all the earth do right" (Gen. 18:25)?

And "you shall know!" Wait for the "hereafter" revelation! An earthly father puzzles not the ear of infancy with hard sayings and involved problems. He waits for the manhood of being, and then unfolds all. So it is with God! We are now in our youth—children lisping in earthly infancy a knowledge of His ways. We shall learn "the deep things of God" (1 Cor. 2:10) in the manhood of eternity! Christ now often shows Himself only "behind the lattice" (Song 2:9)—a glimpse and He is gone! But the day is coming when we shall "see Him as He is" (1 John 3:2)—when every dark hieroglyphic in the Roll of Providence will be interpreted and expounded!

It is unfair to criticize the half-finished picture—to censure or condemn the half-developed plan. God's plans are here in embryo. "We see," says Samuel Rutherford (1600-1661), "but broken links of the chains of His Providence. Let the former work His own clay in what frame He pleaseth." But a flood of light will break upon us from the sapphire Throne—"In your light we see light" (Ps. 36:9). The "need be," muffled as a secret now, will be confided to us *then*, and become luminous with love.

Perhaps we may not even have to wait until eternity for the realization of this promise. We may experience its fulfilment here. We not infrequently find, even in this present world, mysterious dispensations issuing in un-looked-for blessing. Jacob would never have seen Joseph had he not parted with Benjamin. Often would the believer never have seen the true *Joseph* had he not been called on to part with his best beloved! His language at the time is that of the patriarch, "I am indeed bereaved . . . all these things are against me" (Gen. 42:36). But the things which he imagined to be so adverse, have proved the means of leading him to see the heavenly King "in his beauty" (Isa. 33:17) before he dies. Much is sent to "humble us and to prove us" (Ps. 66:10). It may not do us good *now*, but it is promised to do so "at the latter end" (Job 42:12).

I shall not dictate to my God what His ways should be. The patient does not dictate to his Physician. He does not reject and refuse the prescription because it is nauseous; He knows it is for his good, and takes it on trust. It is for faith to repose in whatever God appoints. Let me not wrong His love or dishonor His faithfulness by supposing that there is one needless or redundant drop in the cup which His loving wisdom has mingled. "Now we know in part; hut *then* shall we know even as also we are known" (1 Cor. 13:12)!

> "And it shall come to pass,
> when I bring a cloud over the earth,
> that the bow shall be seen in the cloud."

> *He leadeth me, O blessèd thought!*
> *O words with heav'nly comfort fraught!*
> *Whate'er I do, where'er I be*
> *Still 'tis God's hand that leadeth me.*
>
> *Sometimes mid scenes of deepest gloom,*
> *Sometimes where Eden's bowers bloom,*
> *By waters still, over troubled sea,*
> *Still 'tis His hand that leadeth me.*

(Taken from *He Leadeth Me* by Joseph H. Gilmore, 1834-1918)

- *Day 15* -

The Choosing Place

"I have chosen you in the furnace of affliction."
Isaiah 48:10

The furnace of affliction! It is God's meeting place with His people. "I have chosen you," says He. "There I will keep you, until the purifying process is complete; and, if need be, in a chariot of fire I will carry you to Heaven!"

Some fires are for destruction, but this is for purification. He, the Refiner is sitting by the furnace regulating the flames, tempering the heat; not the least filing of the gold but what is precious to Him! The bush is burning with fire, but He is in the midst of it—a living God in the bush—a living Savior in the furnace!

And has not this been the method of His dealing with His faithful people in every age: first, trial—then, blessings; first, difficulties—then, deliverances. There is Egypt, plagues, darkness, brick kilns, the Red Sea, forty years of desert privations—then *Canaan*! First, there is the burning fiery furnace; *then*, the vision of "one like the Son of God" (Dan. 3:25). Or, as with Elijah on Carmel, the answer is first by fire, and then by rain. First, the fiery trial, then the gentle descent of the Spirit's influences, coming down "like rain upon the mown grass, and as showers that water the earth" (Ps. 72:6).

Believer, be it yours to ask, Are my trials sanctified? Are they making me holier, purer, better, more meek, more gentle, more heavenly-minded, more Savior-like? Seek to "glorify God in the fires" (Isa. 24:15). Patience is a grace which the angels cannot manifest. It is a flower of earth, it blooms not in Paradise; it requires tribulation for its exercise; it is nurtured only amid wind, and hail, and storm. By patient, unmurmuring submission, remember, you, a poor sinner, can thus magnify your God in a way the loftiest angelic natures cannot do! He is taking you to the inner chambers of His covenant faithfulness. His design is to purge away your dross, to bring you forth from the furnace reflecting His own image, and fitted for glory!

Those intended for great usefulness are much in the refining pot. "His children," says William Romaine (1714-1795), "have found suffering times happy times. They never have such nearness to their Father, such holy freedom with Him, and such heavenly refreshment with Him, as under the cross." "Beloved, think it not strange concerning the fiery trial which is to try you . . . but rejoice" (1 Pet. 4:12-13).

> "And it shall come to pass,
> when I bring a cloud over the earth,
> that the bow shall be seen in the cloud."

Give to the winds thy fears,

The Choosing Place

Hope and be undismayed.
God hears thy sighs and counts thy tears,
God shall lift up thy head.

Through waves and clouds and storms,
He gently clears thy way;
Wait thou His time; so shall this night
Soon end in joyous day.

Still heavy is thy heart?
Still sinks thy spirit down?
Cast off the world, let fear depart
Bid every care be gone.

.   .   .

Leave to His sovereign sway
To choose and to command;
So shalt thou, wondering, own that way,
How wise, how strong this hand.

Far, far above thy thought,
His counsel shall appear,
When fully He the work hath wrought,
That caused thy needless fear.

(Taken from *Give to the Winds Thy Fears* by Paul Gerhardt, 1607-1676)

- *Day 16* -

Mourning Ended

"The days of your mourning shall be ended."
Isaiah 60:20

The believer has "mourning days." The place of his sojourn is a valley of tears. Adam went weeping from his paradise; we go weeping on the way to ours. But, pilgrim of grief, your tears are numbered. A few more aching sighs, a few more gloomy clouds and the eternal sun shall burst on you, whose radiance shall nevermore be obscured!

Life may be to you one long "valley of Baca" (Ps. 84:6), a protracted scene of weeping! But soon you shall hear the sweet chimes wafted from the towers of the new Jerusalem: "Enter into the joy of your Lord" (Matt. 25:21); "The Lord God shall wipe away all tears from off all faces" (Isa. 25:8).

"The *days* of your mourning!" It is a consoling thought that all these days are appointed, meted out, numbered. "Unto you it is *given*," says the apostle, "to suffer" (Phil. 1:29). Yes, and if you are a child of the covenant, your mourning days are days of special privilege, intended to be fraught with blessing. To the unbeliever, they are earnests of everlasting woe; to the believer, they are preludes and precursors of eternal glory! Affliction to the one is the cloud without the Bow; to the other, it is the cloud radiant and lustrous with gospel promise and gospel hope!

Reader, are you now one of the many members of the family of sorrow? Be comforted! Soon the long night watch will be over—pain, sickness, weakness, and weariness. Soon the windows of the soul will be no more darkened. Soon you shall have nothing to be delivered from; your present losses and crosses will turn into eternal gains—the dews of the night of weeping (nature's teardrops) will come to sparkle like beautiful gems in the morning of immortality! Soon the Master's footsteps will be heard, saying, "The days of your mourning are ended," and you shall take off your sackcloth, and be girded with gladness.

Up to that moment, your life may have been one long *day* of mourning, but once past the golden portals, and the eye can be dim no more, the very fountain of weeping will be dried! The period of your mourning is counted by "days"—of your eternal rejoicing by eras and cycles! "Why are you then cast down, my soul, and why are you disquieted within me? Hope in God!" (Ps. 42:5).

I will gaze through my tears on this celestial rainbow, and sing this "song in the night" (Ps. 77:6), which the God, who is to wipe my tears away, has put into my lips: "And there shall be no more death, neither sorrow, nor crying, neither shall there be any more pain: for the former things are passed away" (Rev. 21:4).

"And it shall come to pass,

when I bring a cloud over the earth,
that the bow shall be seen in the cloud."

When all my labors and trials are o'er,
And I am safe on that beautiful shore,
Just to be near the dear Lord I adore,
Will through the ages be glory for me.

When, by the gift of His infinite grace,
I am accorded in Heaven a place,
Just to be there and to look on His face,
Will through the ages be glory for me.

(Taken from *O That Will Be Glory* by Charles H. Gabriel, 1856-1932)

- *Day 17* -

The Abiding Friend

"I will never leave you, nor forsake you."
Hebrews 13:5

No human friend can say so. The closest and clearest of earthly links may be broken; yea, I have been broken. Distance may part, time estrange, the grave sunder. Loving earthly looks may only greet you now in mute smiles from the portrait on the wall. But here is an unfainting, unvarying, unfailing Friend. Sorrowing one, amid the wreck of earthly joys which you may be even now bewailing, here is a message sent to you from your God: "I will never leave you, nor forsake you!" Your gourd has withered (see Jonah 4:7), but He who gave it to you remains! Surrender yourself to His disposal. He wishes to show you His present sufficiency for your happiness.

As often as your heart in silence and sadness weaves its plaintive lament, "Joseph is not, and Simeon is not" (Gen 42:36), think of Him who has promised to set "the solitary in families" (Ps. 68:6), and to "give unto them a place and a name better than of sons or of daughters" (Isa. 56:5) Alone? You are not alone! Turn in self-oblivion to Jesus. It is not, it cannot be "night," if He, "the Sun of your soul," be ever near! In the morning, He comes with the earliest beam that visits your room. When the curtains of night close around you, He, to whom "the darkness and the light are both alike" (Ps. 139:12) is at your side! In the stillness of night, when in your wakeful moments, the visions of the departed flit before you like shadows on the wall, He, the unslumbering Shepherd of Israel, is tending your bed, and whispering in your ear, "Fear not, for I am with you" (Isa. 41:10).

Your experience may be that of Paul, "All forsook me!" But, like him, also, you will doubtless be able to add in the extremity of your sorrow, "Notwithstanding the Lord stood with me, and strengthened me" (2 Tim. 4:16-17)! He can compensate by His own loving presence, for every earthly loss. Without the consciousness of His friendship and love, the smallest trial will crush you. With Him in your trial, supporting and sustaining you under it, (yea, coming in the place of those you mourn), you will have an infinite and inexhaustible portion for a finite and mutable one. Many a cloud is there without a bow in nature—but never in Grace. Every sorrow has its corresponding and counterpart comfort: "In the multitude of the [sorrows] that I had in my heart, your comforts have refreshed my soul" (Ps. 94:19).

If in the midnight of your grief your earthly sun appears to have set forever, an inner, but not less real sunshine, lights up your stricken heart. The stream of life may have been poisoned at its source, but blessed be His name if it has driven you to say, "All my springs are *in* You" (Ps. 87:7)! "The Lord is my portion, says my soul; therefore will I hope in Him" (Lam. 3:24)!

The Abiding Friend

"And it shall come to pass,
when I bring a cloud over the earth,
that the bow shall be seen in the cloud."

Sun of my soul, Thou Savior dear,
It is not night if Thou be near;
O may no earthborn cloud arise
To hide Thee from Thy servant's eyes.

When the soft dews of kindly sleep
My wearied eyelids gently steep,
Be my last thought, how sweet to rest
Forever on my Savior's breast.

(Taken from *Sun of My Soul* by John Keble, 1792-1866)

- *Day 18* -

Unwilling Discipline

"For He does not afflict willingly nor
grieve the children of men."
Lamentations 3:33

In our seasons of trial, when under some inscrutable dispensation, how apt is the murmuring thought to rise in our hearts: "All things are against me" (Gen. 42:36). Might not this over- whelming blow have been spared? Might not this dark cloud, which has shadowed my heart and my home with sadness, have been averted? Might not the accompaniments of my trial have been less severe? "Has God forgotten to be gracious" (Ps. 77:9)?

No, these afflictions are errands of mercy in disguise! "For he does not afflict willingly." There is nothing capricious or arbitrary about God's dealings. Unutterable tenderness is the character of all His allotments! The world may wound by unkindness. Trusted friends may become treacherous. A brother may speak with unnecessary harshness and severity, but the Lord is "abundant in goodness and in truth" (Ex. 34:6). He appoints no needless pang. When be appears like Joseph to "speak roughly" (Gen. 423:7), there are gentle undertones of love. The stern accents are assumed, because He has precious lessons that could not otherwise have been taught!

Ah! be assured there is some deep *necessity* in all He does. In our calendars of sorrow we may put this luminous mark against every trying hour, "It was needed!" Some redundant branch in the tree required pruning. Some wheat required to be cast overboard to lighten the ship and avert further disaster. Mourning one, He might have dealt far otherwise with you! He might have cut you down as a fruitless, worthless cumberer! He might have abandoned you to drift, disowned and unpiloted on the rocks of destruction, joined to your idols! He might have left you *alone* to settle on your lees, and forfeit your eternal bliss! But He loved you better. It was kindness, infinite kindness, which blighted your fairest blossoms, and hedged up your way with thorns. "Without this hedge of thorns," says Richard Baxter (1615-1691), "on the right hand and on the left, we should hardly be able to keep the way to Heaven."

We, in our blind unbelief, may speak of trials we imagine might have been spared, chastisements that are unnecessarily severe. But the day is coming when every step of the Lord's procedure will be vindicated; when we shall own and recognize each separate experience of sorrow to have been an unspeakably precious and important period in the history of the soul. Yes! child of God. The messenger of affliction has an olive-branch in one hand—a love-token plucked from the bowers of paradise—and in the other, a chalice mingled by One too loving and gracious to insert one needless ingredient of sorrow! Remember, every drop of wrath in that cup was exhausted by a surety-Savior. In taking it into your hand, be it yours to extract support and consolation from what so mightily sustained a Greater

Sufferer in a more awful hour: "The cup which my Father has given me, shall I not drink it?" (John 18:11).

> "And it shall come to pass,
> when I bring a cloud over the earth,
> that the bow shall be seen in the cloud."

God moves in a mysterious way
His wonders to perform;
He plants His footsteps in the sea
And rides upon the storm.

Deep in unfathomable mines
Of never failing skill
He treasures up His bright designs
And works His sovereign will.

Ye fearful saints, fresh courage take;
The clouds ye so much dread
Are big with mercy and shall break
In blessings on your head.

Judge not the Lord by feeble sense,
But trust Him for His grace;
Behind a frowning providence
He hides a smiling face.

(Taken from *God Moves in a Mysterious Way*
by William Cowper, 1731-1800)

- *Day 19* -

Death Vanquished

"I am he that lives, and was dead; and, behold, I am alive forevermore. Amen; and have the keys of hell and of death."
Revelation 1:18

An enthroned Savior speaks! "I" says He, "am he that lives!" (or, "the Living One"). Others have passed away, but I ever live, and ever love! I am now living—a personal Savior—Christ your very life!

Are you stooping over some treasured house of clay, which the whirlwind has made a mass of ruins? I roused the whirlwind from its chamber, appointed the startling dispensation, I ordered the shroud, and prepared the grave! Let not accident, chance, fate, enter into the vocabulary of your sorrow. I am the Lord of death as well as of life, I have the keys of Hades and of the grave suspended at my girdle. The tomb is never unlocked but by Me. Let others talk of the might of the King of Terrors. He has no might but by permission.

More than this, mourning one! "I *was* dead. I myself once entered that gloomy portico! I sanctified and consecrated it by my presence! I was a tenant of the tomb. This now glorified body was once laid by human hands in a borrowed grave!" Can you dread to walk the valley trodden by your Lord, to encounter the last enemy, which He fought and conquered.

Death!—it has been converted by Him into a parenthesis in endless life. "I am He that was dead!" "I am He that lives!"

What more could the Christian desire than this twofold assurance? On the day of atonement of old, the blood was sprinkled alike on the floor and on the mercy seat. The voice of blood arose from the floor below, and the mercy seat above. So it is with the voice of our Elder Brother's blood. It cried first from earth beneath, and now from Heaven. His dying love is now ever-living—imperishable and immutable as His own being!

As the bow in the material firmament can never cease to appear, so long as the present laws of nature continue, and there is a sun in the heavens, so the Bow of the everlasting covenant, and all its blessings, can only fail when Christ, the Sun of Righteousness, ceases to shine, and ceases to be! With such a Bow overarching the future, one limb resting amid the cloud-lands of life, the other melting its hues into the deeper shadows of the valley of death, "I will fear no evil: for thou Savior God, are with me, your rod and your staff they comfort me" (see Ps. 23:4).

> "And it shall come to pass,
> when I bring a cloud over the earth,
> that the bow shall be seen in the cloud."

Death Vanquished

The King of love my shepherd is,
whose goodness faileth never.
I nothing lack if I am his,
and he is mine forever.

Where streams of living water flow,
my ransomed soul he leadeth;
and where the verdant pastures grow,
with food celestial feedeth.

.   .   .

In death's dark vale I fear no ill,
with thee, dear Lord, beside me;
thy rod and staff my comfort still,
thy cross before to guide me.

(Taken from *King of My Love* by H. W. Baker, 1821-1877)

- Day 20 -

The Greatest Gift

"He that spared not His own Son, but delivered him up for us all,
how shall he not with him also freely give us all things."
Romans 8:32

These are amazing words! God, the infinite God, identifying Himself (so to speak) with the experiences of human sorrow; silencing every murmur with the unanswerable argument: "I spared not my own Son." "I gave my Greatest gift for you, will you not cheerfully surrender your best to Me? Can you refuse after this unspeakable gift of My love, to trust Me in lesser things?" The Greater gift may surely well be a pledge for the bestowment of all needed subordinate good!

He promises to give "all things"— these "all things" are in *His* hand. They will be selected and allotted by His loving wisdom; crosses as well as comforts, sorrows and tears, as well as smiles and joys. Mourning one, this very trial which now dims your eye is one of these "all things." Trust His faithfulness. He would as soon wound the Son of His love as wound you! "How shall He not give?" There is a blessed impossibility, after the bestowment of the

Gift of gifts, that He will inflict one unnecessary trial, or withhold one needed blessing. Think of His love when He offered His Isaac on the altar. It is the same at this hour—infinite—immutable. Yes, we may well be reconciled, even to the denial of earthly blessedness, because ordered by Him who gave Jesus! Lying meekly in the arms of His mercy, be it ours to say in filial confidence: "Lord, anything with your love, anything but your frown!"

"All things." The whole range of human wants and necessities is known to Him. The care He invites me to cast upon Him is "all my care"; the need, "all my need!" This is His own special promise, "And God is able to make all grace abound toward you; that you, always having all sufficiency in all things, may abound to every good work." (2 Cor. 9:8). He will give me nothing and deny me nothing, but what is for my good. Let me not question the appointments of infinite wisdom. Let me not wound Him by one dishonoring doubt. Let me lean upon Him in little things as well as in great things. After the pledge of His love in Jesus, nothing can come wrong that comes from His hands! If tempted at times to harbor some unkind misgivings, let the sight of the cross dispel it.

Looking to the Bow in the cloud gleaming with the words, "Who loved me, and gave Himself for me" (Gal. 2:20), be it mine to say,

Lord, though Thou bend my spirit low,
Love only will I see;
The very hand that strikes the blow,
Was wounded once for me.

> "And it shall come to pass,
> when I bring a cloud over the earth,

that the bow shall be seen in the cloud."

Day by day and with each passing moment,
Strength I find to meet my trials here;
Trusting in my Father's wise bestowment,
I've no cause for worry or for fear.

He whose heart is kind beyond all measure
Gives unto each day what He deems best—
Lovingly, its part of pain and pleasure,
Mingling toil with peace and rest.

Ev'ry day the Lord Himself is near me
With a special mercy for each hour;
All my cares He fain would bear, and cheer me,
He whose name is Counselor and Pow'r.

The protection of His child and treasure
Is a charge that on Himself He laid;
"As thy days, thy strength shall be in measure,"
This the pledge to me He made.

Help me then in ev'ry tribulation
So to trust Thy promises, O Lord,
That I lose not faith's sweet consolation
Offered me within Thy holy Word.

Help me, Lord, when toil and trouble meeting,
E'er to take, as from a father's hand,
One by one, the days, the moments fleeting,
Till I reach the promised land.

(*Day by Day* by Karolina Sandell-Berg, 1832-1903)

- *Day 21* -

Sleeping and Waking

"Them also which sleep in Jesus will God bring with him."
1 Thessalonians 4:14

Or, as these words have been rendered, "Them also which are *laid asleep in Jesus.*"

We bid an earthly friend "Good night" in the pleasing expectation of meeting next morning. The saints are "laid asleep" in the grave of Jesus, in the sure and certain hope of meeting Him in the morning of immortality!

Child of God, weep not for those who have "departed to be with Christ." It is with them "far better." Think not of them as *gone.* That is a word taken from the vocabulary of death, and which, it is to be feared, is often employed with many in the heathen sense of *annihilation.* Seek not "the living among the dead" (Luke 24:5). Think rather that the last sigh was scarce over on earth, when the song was begun in Heaven. The Spirit winged its arrow-flight among ministering seraphim. Hear that voice stealing down in the soft whisper of Heaven's music, and saying, "If you loved me ye would rejoice, because I said, I go unto my Father" (John 14:28)!

The body, the casket of this immortal jewel, is left for a season to the dishonors of the tomb. But it is only for a brief night watch. That dust is precious, because redeemed. Body as well as soul was purchased by the life-blood of Immanuel. Angels guard these slumbering ashes, and the day is coming when God shall "send His angels with a great sound of a trumpet, and they shall gather together His elect from the four winds, from one end of Heaven to the other" (Matt. 24:31).

Oh, if there be "joy among the angels of God over one sinner that repents" (Luke 15:10), what shall be the joy of those blessed beings over the myriads of rising dead, hastening at their summons to their crowns and thrones! Christian mourner, "Your brother shall rise again" (John 11:23). Wish him not back amid the storms of the wilderness. Be thankful rather that the wheat is no longer out in the tempest and rain, but safely garnered, eternally housed. You would not, surely, if you could, weep that blessed one back from glory and ask him to unlearn Heaven's language, and be once more involved in the dust of battle, would you? No, rather "rejoice in hope of the glory of God" (Rom. 5:2). Death is not an eternal sleep. "Yet a little while, and He that shall come will come, and will not tarry" (Heb. 10:37). Jesus is now whispering in your ear the glorious secret hid from ages and generations, and which, was left to Him, as the Abolisher of Death, to disclose: "Your dead shall live; together with my dead body shall they arise" (Isa. 26:19). He is pointing you onward to that hour of jubilee, when the summons shall be addressed to all His sleeping saints, "Awake and sing, you that dwell in dust" (Isa. 26:19)!

Oh happy day! when I shall see my Savior God in all the glories of His exalted humanity; and *with* Him, the once loved and lost, now the loved and glorified, never to be lost again! "The Lord my God shall come, and all the saints with you" (Zech. 14:5). Not one shall be wanting. In concert with those whose tongues are now silent on earth, we shall then unite in the lofty anthem, sung by the ingathered Church triumphant, "O death, where is your sting? O grave, where is your victory? Thanks be to God, who gives us the victory through the Lord Jesus Christ" (1 Cor. 15:55, 57).

> "And it shall come to pass,
> when I bring a cloud over the earth,
> that the bow shall be seen in the cloud."

Safe in the arms of Jesus, safe on His gentle breast,
There by His love o'ershaded, sweetly my soul shall rest.
Hark! 'tis the voice of angels, borne in a song to me.
Over the fields of glory, over the jasper sea.

. . .

Jesus, my heart's dear Refuge, Jesus has died for me;
Firm on the Rock of Ages, ever my trust shall be.
Here let me wait with patience, wait till the night is over;
Wait till I see the morning break on the golden shore.

(Taken from *Safe in the Arms of Jesus* by Fanny Crosby, 1820-1915)

- *Day 22* -

Invisible Harmonies

*"We know that all things work together for good
to them that love God, to them who are the
called according to his purpose."*
Romans 8:28

We are apt to "limit the Holy One of Israel" (Ps. 78:41), and to say, "*Some* things have worked together for our good." God says, "*All* things!"—joys, sorrows, crosses, losses, prosperity, adversity, health, sickness; the gourd bestowed, and the gourd withered (see Jonah 4:7); the cup full, and the cup emptied; the lingering sick bed, the early grave!

Often, indeed, would sight and sense lead us to doubt the reality of the promise. We can see, in many things, scarce a dim reflection of love. Useful lives taken—blossoms prematurely plucked—spiritual props removed—benevolent schemes blown upon. But the apostle does not say, "We see," but "We know." It is the province of faith to trust God in the dark. The uninitiated and undiscerning cannot understand or explain the revolutions and dependencies of the varied wheels in a complicated machine, but they have confidence in the wisdom of the artificer, that all is designed to work out some great and useful end.

Be it ours to write over every mysterious dealing, "This also comes from the Lord of hosts, who is wonderful in counsel and excellent in working" (Isa. 28:29)! Let us "be still and know that He is God" (Ps. 46:10). "We have a wonderful advertisement of a Physician from the Spirit of Truth," says Lady Powerscourt (1800-1836), "'who healeth all thy diseases.' He requires but one thing, to take *all* He has prescribed, bitter as well as sweet!"

He will yet vindicate His own rectitude and faithfulness in our trials; our own souls will be made the better for them; He himself will be glorified in them. "Doubt not my love," He seems to say, "The day is coming when you shall have all mysteries explained, all secrets unraveled, and this very trial demonstrated to be one of the 'all things' working together for your good." "Men see not the bright light in the clouds" (Job 37:21), but it shall come to pass that at evening time it shall be *light*" (Zech. 14:7).

> "And it shall come to pass,
> when I bring a cloud over the earth,
> that the bow shall be seen in the cloud."

In Heavenly love abiding, no change my heart shall fear.
And safe in such confiding, for nothing changes here.
The storm may roar without me, my heart may low be laid,
But God is round about me, and can I be dismayed?

Wherever He may guide me, no want shall turn me back.

My Shepherd is beside me, and nothing can I lack.
His wisdom ever waking, His sight is never dim.
He knows the way He's taking, and I will walk with Him.

Green pastures are before me, which yet I have not seen.
Bright skies will soon be over me, where darkest clouds have
    been.
My hope I cannot measure, my path to life is free.
My Savior has my treasure, and He will walk with me.

(*In Heavenly Love Abiding* by Anna L. Waring, 1823-1910)

- *Day 23* -

The Unchanging Name

"Jesus Christ, the same yesterday, and today, and forever."
Hebrews 13:8

ALL is changing here. Life is a kaleidoscope, made up of shifting forms: new scenes, new tastes, new feelings, new associations; it is an alternation of cloud and sunshine, tempest and calm. Its joys are like the air bubbles on the stream, tinted with sunlight: we touch them and they are gone! We witness the vacant seats in our sanctuaries, vacant seats at our home-hearths, the music of well-known voices hushed. Often just when we imagine we have at last obtained a stable footing, the scaffolding gives way, the prop on which for a lifetime we had been leaning fails, and we feel ourselves out amid the pitiless storm.

But is there nothing stable amid all this mutability? Is there nothing secure and abiding amid these fleeting shadows? Yes! Jesus is without any variableness. Eighteen hundred years have rolled by since He left our world. The world has changed, but He is to this hour the same. We can follow Him through all His wondrous pilgrimage of love on earth. We can behold penitence crouching at His feet, and sent away forgiven; sorrow tracking His footsteps with tears, and sent away with her tears dried and her wounded spirit healed; pain and sickness pleading with pallid lip and wasted feature; and disease, at His omnipotent mandate, taking wings to itself and fleeing away! And He who is now on the heavenly Throne is "that same Jesus." His ascension-glories have not changed His changeless heart or alienated His affections. In Him we have a Rock which the billows of adversity cannot shake. The spent fury of the chafing waves may reach us no more—and this only endearing the security and value of the abiding Refuge!

How often does God rouse the storm to drive us from all creature confidences to the only stable One! How often does He poison and pollute the stream to lead us to seek the everlasting Fountainhead!

We may have lost much, but if we have found You, O blessed Jesus, we possess infinitely more than we have forfeited. We can glory in the persuasion that nothing can ever separate us from Your love. Our best earthly friends, a look may alienate; an unintentional word may estrange; the grave must sunder. But "the LORD lives, and blessed be my Rock, and let the God of my salvation be exalted" (Ps. 18:46), and what You have been *yesterday*—yea, from everlasting ages—You are *this day*, and You shall be *forever and ever*! We can look to the Bow of Your promises, and behold all of them in You are "yes and amen" (2 Cor. 1:20)! You are addressing us from Your throne in glory—that throne spoken of in Revelation as encircled with the rainbow of emerald (the emblem of perpetuity), and saying, "Fear not, I am He that lives, and was dead, and behold I am alive forevermore" (Rev. 1:18). "Because I live, you shall live also" (John 14:19)!

The Unchanging Name

"And it shall come to pass,
when I bring a cloud over the earth,
that the bow shall be seen in the cloud."

Abide with me; fast falls the eventide;
The darkness deepens; Lord with me abide.
When other helpers fail and comforts flee,
Help of the helpless, O abide with me.

Swift to its close ebbs out life's little day;
Earth's joys grow dim; its glories pass away;
Change and decay in all around I see;
O Thou who changest not, abide with me.

.   .   .

I need Thy presence every passing hour.
What but Thy grace can foil the tempter's power?
Who, like Thyself, my guide and stay can be?
Through cloud and sunshine, Lord, abide with me.

Hold Thou Thy cross before my closing eyes;
Shine through the gloom and point me to the skies.
Heaven's morning breaks, and earth's vain shadows flee;
In life, in death, O Lord, abide with me.

(Taken from *Abide With Me* by Henry F. Lyte, 1793-1847)

- *Day 24* -

Strength for the Day

"As your days, so shall your strength be."
Deuteronomy 33:25

Believer, have you not felt it so? Have you not found plants distilling balm, growing beside sorrow's path, comforts and supports vouchsafed, which were undreamt of until the dreaded cloud had burst, and the day of trial had come? Trouble not yourself regarding an unknown and veiled future, but cast all your cares on God. "Our sandals," says a saint now in glory, "are proof against the roughest path."

He whose name is "the God of all grace" (1 Pet. 5:10) is better than His word. He will be found equal to all the emergencies of His people, enough for each moment and each hour as they come. He never takes us to the bitter Marah streams (see Ex. 15:22-24), but that He reveals also the hidden branch. Paul was hurled down from the third heavens to endure the smarting of his "thorn," but he rises like a giant from his fall, exulting in the sustaining grace of an "all-sufficient God" (see 2 Cor. 12:7-9).

The beautiful peculiarity in this promise is, that God proportions His grace to the nature and the season of trial. He does not forestall or advance a supply of grace, but when the needed season and exigency comes, then the appropriate strength and support are imparted. He does not send the Bow before the Cloud, but when the Cloud appears, the Bow is seen in it! He gives sustaining grace for a trying day, and dying grace for a dying day.

Reader, do not morbidly brood on the future. Live on the promise! When the morrow comes with its trials, Jesus will come with the morrow, and with its trials too. Present grace is enough for present necessity. Trust God for the future. Aye, honor Him, not by anticipating trial, but by confiding in His faithfulness, and crediting His assurance, that no temptation will be sent greater than we are able to bear. Even if you should see fresh clouds returning after the rain, be ready to say, "I will fear no evil: for *Thou* art with me" (Ps. 23:4)!

Insufficient you are of yourself for any trial, but "your sufficiency is of God" (2 Cor. 3:5). The promise is not "*Your* grace," but "*My* grace is sufficient." Oh, trust His "all sufficiency in all things!" Jehovah-Jireh, "the Lord will provide" (see Gen. 22:8, 14). See written over every trying hour of the future, "So shall your strength be!"

> "And it shall come to pass,
> when I bring a cloud over the earth,
> that the bow shall be seen in the cloud."

Though troubles assail us and dangers affright,

Though friends should all fail us and foes all unite,
Yet one thing secures us, whatever betide,
The promise assures us, The Lord will provide.

The birds, without garner or storehouse, are fed;
From them let us learn to trust God for our bread.
His saints what is fitting shall ne'er be denied
So long as 'tis written, The Lord will provide.

We all may, like ships, by tempest be tossed
On perilous deeps, but can not be lost;
Though Satan enrages the wind and the tide,
Yet Scripture engages, The Lord will provide.

. . .

No strength of our own and no goodness we claim;
Yet, since we have known of the Savior's great name,
In this our strong tower for safety we hide:
The Lord is our power, The Lord will provide.

When life sinks apace, and death is in view,
The word of His grace shall comfort us through,
Not fearing or doubting, with Christ on our side,
We hope to die shouting, The Lord will provide.

(Taken from *Though Troubles Assail Us* by John Newton, 1725-1807)

- Day 25 -

The Grave Spoiled

*"I will ransom them from the power of the grave; I will
redeem them from death: O death, I will be your
plagues: O Grave, I will be your destruction."*
Hosea 13:14

Christian, the Grave is lighted with Immanuel's love! The darkest
of all clouds—that which rests over the land of Hades—has the
brightest Bow in it. These gloomy portals are not to hold your loved
and lost forever. The land of forgetfulness, where your buried treasures lie, is not a winter of unbroken darkness and desolation. A glorious springtime of revival is promised, "when the mortal shall have
put on immortality, and the corruptible shall be clothed with incor-
ruption" (see 1 Cor. 15:54).

The resurrection of the body! It is the climax of the work of Jesus—
its culminating glory. St. Paul represents a longing Church—as
"waiting for the adoption, the redemption of our body" (Rom.
8:23). It was the preeminent theme of his preaching: "He preached
unto them Jesus, and the resurrection of the dead" (Acts 17:18). It
was the loved article in his creed, which engrossed his own holiest

aspirations, "If by any means I might attain unto the resurrection of the dead" (Phil. 3:11). It was the grand solace he administered to other mourners. It is not when speaking of the immediate bliss of the departed spirit at the hour of death, but it is when dwelling on "the last trump"—the dead "rising incorruptible" and "caught up," in their resurrection bodies "to meet the Lord," that he says, "Wherefore comfort one another with these words" (see 1 Thess. 4:16-18).

Blessed day—the great Easter of creation—the dawn of the Sabbath morn, the Jubilee of a triumphant Church! Christian mourner, go not to the grave to weep there. Every particle of that earthly dust is redeemed by the oblation of Calvary; and the great Abolisher of death is only awaiting the ingathering of His elect, to give the commission to His archangels regarding all His saints, which He gave of old regarding one, "Loose him, and let him go" (John 11:44)!

And who can imagine the glory of these Resurrection bodies, reunited to their glorified companion-spirits, fashioned like their Lord's—every sense, every faculty—purified, sublimated, infused with holiness; emulous with ardor in His service, eager to execute His will; retaining, it may be, the personal identities of earth, the old features worn in the nether valley. Now, it is reunited to death-divided friends in ties which know no dissolution, no trace of grief lingering on their countenances, no accents of sorrow trembling on their tongues! The Lamb, in the midst of the throne, *leading* them and *feeding* them; climbing along with them, steep by steep, in the path of life, and saying at each ascending step in the endless progression, "I will show you greater things than these" (John 1:50).

Meanwhile, He has Himself risen as the pledge of this resurrection of all His people. The Great Sheaf has been waved before the throne as the Earnest of the mighty harvest, "Christ the firstfruits; afterward they that are Christ's at His coming" (1 Cor. 15:23). "Blessed and holy is he that has part in the first resurrection" (Rev. 20:6).

> "And it shall come to pass,
> when I bring a cloud over the earth,
> that the bow shall be seen in the cloud."

Jesus lives, and so shall I.
Death! thy sting is gone forever!
He who deigned for me to die,
Lives, the bands of death to sever.
He shall raise me from the dust:
Jesus is my Hope and Trust.

Jesus lives, and reigns supreme,
And, his kingdom still remaining,
I shall also be with him,
Ever living, ever reigning.
God has promised: be it must:
Jesus is my Hope and Trust.

(Taken from *Jesus Lives, and So Shall I*
by Christian F. Gellert, 1715-1769)

- *Day 26* -

Everlasting Love

"I have loved you with an everlasting love: therefore
with loving-kindness have I drawn you."
Jeremiah 31:3

Believer, are you tempted now to doubt His love? Are His footsteps lost amid the night shadows through which He is now leading you? Remember, He had His eye upon you before the birth of time; yea, from all eternity! What appears to you now some sudden capricious exercise of His power or sovereignty, is the determination and decree of "everlasting love." "I loved you," He seems to say, "suffering one, into this affliction; I will love you through it; and when my designs regarding you are completed, I will show you that the love which is 'from everlasting, is to everlasting.'"

Child of God, if there is a ripple now agitating the surface of the stream, trace it up to this Fountainhead of love. God is faithful. He cannot deny Himself. He must have some wise end to serve, if some dark clouds are now intercepting these gracious beams. "'For a small moment I have forsaken you; but with great mercies will I gather you. In a little wrath I hid my face from you for a moment;

but with everlasting kindness will I have mercy on you,' says the Lord your Redeemer. 'For this is as the waters of Noah unto me: for as I have sworn that the waters of Noah should no more go over the earth, so have I sworn that I would not be wroth with you, nor rebuke you. For the mountains shall depart, and the hills be removed; but my kindness shall not depart from you, neither shall the covenant of my peace be removed,' says the Lord that has mercy on you" (Isa. 54:7-10).

God sets His Bow in the dark sky; and as if it were not enough that His *people* should look upon it and take comfort in its many and varied promises—He Himself graciously becomes a party in gazing on the covenant pledge: "And the Bow shall be in the cloud, and *I shall look upon it*, that I may remember the everlasting covenant" (Gen. 9:16). He puts Himself (so to speak) in mind of His own everlasting love! In His saints' dark and cloudy day, when they imagine that *their* eyes are alone resting on the tokens of covenant faithfulness, the eye of a covenant-keeping God is resting upon them too. "I will look upon my own Promises," He seems to say, "they shall be memorials to Myself of My purposes, My unchanging mercy." Nor is this love merely a general indiscriminate affection. The motto- verse speaks of each individual member of the covenant family! "O my Father," says Madam Guyon (1648-1717), "it seems to me sometimes as if Thou didst forget every other being in order to think only of my faithless and ungrateful heart."

Let us seek to view our trials as so many cords of loving-kindness, by which our God is seeking to draw us, yea, and will draw us nearer Himself. Who knows what mercy may be bound up in what may seem to us dark and mysterious dispensations? We are apt to misname and misinterpret His ways. We call His dealings severe trials. He calls them "loving-kindnesses."

Drooping saint! let your eyes rest on the Rainbow over-arching the throne of God, spanning from eternity to eternity; and read for your comfort the gracious declaration, "The mercy of the Lord is from everlasting to everlasting upon them that fear him" (Ps. 103:17).

> "And it shall come to pass,
> when I bring a cloud over the earth,
> that the bow shall be seen in the cloud."

> *There's a wideness in God's mercy,*
> *Like the wideness of the sea;*
> *There's a kindness in His justice,*
> *Which is more than liberty.*
>
> . . .
>
> *For the love of God is broader*
> *Than the measure of our mind;*
> *And the heart of the Eternal*
> *Is most wonderfully kind.*

(Taken from *There's a Wideness in God's Mercy*
by Frederick W. Faber, 1814-1863)

- *Day 27* -

Inviolable Attachment

"There is a friend who sticks closer than a brother."
Proverbs 18:24

Close is the tie which binds brother to brother; the companions of infancy, sharers of one another's joys and sorrows; cast in the same human mold; having engraved on their heart of hearts the same hallowed associations of life's early morning.

But the time for separation at last comes. The birds must leave the parents' nest, and try their pinions beyond their native valley. The world's call to work and warfare is imperious. The old homestead, like a dismembered vessel, is broken to pieces; and the inmates, like that vessel's planks, strew far apart the trough of life's ocean. The world's duties sever some; unhappy estrangements at times, may sever others; death, at some time, *must* sever all.

But there is One whose friendship and love circumstances cannot estrange, distance cannot affect, and death cannot destroy. The kindest of earthly relatives may say to us regarding this true Elder Brother, as Boaz said to Ruth, "It is true that I am your near kinsman: howbeit there is a kinsman *nearer* than I" (Ruth 3:12). He is brother, yea, more than brother: Friend, Counsellor, Portion, Physician, Shepherd, all combined! Happy for us, when the old avenues of comfort are closed up, to hear Him, whose faithfulness is unimpeachable, saying, "I will not leave you nor forsake you" (Deut. 31:6). Happy for us when the old moorings give way, to have One safe Anchorage, that cannot be removed or shaken. "I shall now go to sleep," said a remarkable saint, who, driven about with storm and tempest, at last found the safe Shelter—"I shall now go to sleep on the Rock of Ages!"

Tried believer, He has never failed you, and never will. With Him are no altered tones, no fitful affections. The reed may be shaken, but the Rock remains immutable. He is Himself the true "Bow in the cloud." The promises of Scripture, like the varied hues in the natural rainbow, are manifold. But all these promises are "*in* Him" (2 Cor. 1:20). Aye, and it is in the *cloudy day* that this divine encircling Bow most gloriously appears. Never should we have known Christ as the "Brother, born for adversity" (Prov. 17:17) unless *by* adversity.

It is trial that unfolds and develops His infinite worth and preciousness. When the love of earthly friends is buried in the grave, the love of the heavenly Friend shines forth more tenderly than ever. As Jonathan of old, wandering faint and weary in the woods, found honey distilling from a tree and was revived by eating it, so, faint and weary one—wandering amid the tangled thickets and the deep glades of affliction—seat yourself under your "Beloved's shadow with great delight, and let His fruit be pleasant to your taste" (Song 2:3)! This Tree of Life distils a balm for every broken, wounded, bleeding heart—every faint and downcast spirit. Yes, Jesus will make, in this the hour of your loneliness and sorrow, His own life-giving, life-sustaining words and promises, "sweeter also than honey and the honeycomb" (Ps. 19:10). Though now exalted on the throne, inhabiting the praises of eternity, He still manifests the Brother's heart and the Brother's tenderness. "He is not ashamed to call us brothers" (Heb. 2:11).

> "And it shall come to pass,
> when I bring a cloud over the earth,
> that the bow shall be seen in the cloud."

> *Jesus! what a Friend for sinners!*
> *Jesus! Lover of my soul;*
> *Friends may fail me, foes assail me,*
> *He, my Savior, makes me whole.*
>
> .   .   .
>
> *Jesus! what a Help in sorrow!*
> *While the billows over me roll,*
> *Even when my heart is breaking,*
> *He, my Comfort, helps my soul.*

(Taken from *Jesus! What a Friend of Sinners*
by J. Wilbur Chapman, 1859-1918)

- *Day 28* -

The Supporting Presence

"When you pass through the waters, I will be with you;
and through the rivers, they shall not overflow you:
when you walk through the fire, you shall not be
burned, neither shall the flame kindle upon you."
Isaiah 43:2

What a diversity of afflictions in this trial-world—"waters," "streams," "floods," "flames," "fires"! The Christian is here fore-warned that he will encounter these in one of their innumerable phases—whether it be loss of health, loss of wealth, loss of friends, baffled schemes, or blighted hopes.

But, blessed thought, these trials have their limits. The *floods* will not "overflow," the *fires* will not "burn," the *flames* will not "consume." God will "stay His rough wind in the day of His east wind" (Isa. 27:8). He will say, "Thus far shall you go, and no far-ther." And, better still, Jesus will be *in* all these trials, and prove sufficient for them all. We shall hear in the midst "of the great fight of afflictions" (Heb. 10:32) the sound of our Master's footsteps. He Himself has passed through these flames, braved these floods, and bared His guiltless head to these storms. He comes to us as He did to His disciples in the very midst of the tempest, and says, "Be of good cheer: it is I, be not afraid" (Mark 6:50).

Believer, what is your experience? Is it not that of the triumphant Israelites? "They went through the flood on foot: *there* did we rejoice in Him" (Ps. 66:6). "The Flood!" The very scene of your trial, you were able to march boldly through it, unshaken by the threatening waves; yea, with your lips vocal with praise! How this moral heroism—this strange *rejoicing*? It was because the God of the Pillar-cloud was at your side. Your rejoicing was "in Him." He made you "more than conqueror" (Rom. 8:37). You may have many adversaries ranged against you: "tribulation, or distress, or persecution, or famine, nakedness, or peril, or sword" (Rom. 8:35). But there is One in the midst of fires and flames and floods mightier than all; and with Him at your side, you can boldly utter the challenge to the heights above and the depths beneath, "Who shall separate me from the love of Christ?" (Rom. 8:35). "Oh, Sirs!" said Thomas Brooks (1608-1680), "there is in a crucified Jesus something proportionate to all the straits, wants, necessities, and trials of His poor people."

> "And it shall come to pass,
> when I bring a cloud over the earth,
> that the bow shall be seen in the cloud."

Fear not, I am with thee, O be not dismayed,
For I am thy God and will still give thee aid;
I'll strengthen and help thee, and cause thee to stand
Upheld by My righteous, omnipotent hand.

When through the deep waters I call thee to go,
The rivers of woe shall not thee overflow;
For I will be with thee, thy troubles to bless,
And sanctify to thee thy deepest distress.

When through fiery trials thy pathways shall lie,
My grace, all sufficient, shall be thy supply;
The flame shall not hurt thee; I only design
Thy dross to consume, and thy gold to refine.

Even down to old age all My people shall prove
My sovereign, eternal, unchangeable love;
And when hoary hairs shall their temples adorn,
Like lambs they shall still in My bosom be borne.

The soul that on Jesus has leaned for repose,
I will not, I will not desert to its foes;
That soul, though all hell should endeavor to shake,
I'll never, no never, no never forsake.

(Taken from *How Firm a Foundation*; attributed to various authors)

- *Day 29* -

Fellow-Feeling

"We have not an high priest which cannot be touched
with the feeling of our infirmities."
Hebrews 4:15

"As the appearance," says Ezekiel, "of the Bow that is in the cloud in the day of rain, so was the appearance of the brightness round about. This was the appearance of the likeness of the glory of the Lord" (Ezek. 1:28). What an elevating truth. The sympathy of the God-Man-Mediator (the true *Bow* in the cloud)—Jesus in our sorrows! What a source of exalted joy to the suffering and desolate heart! What a green pasture to lie down upon, amid the windy storm and tempest, or in the dark and cloudy day!

The sympathy of man is cheering and comforting, but thus far shall you go, and no farther. It is finite, limited, often selfish. There are nameless and numberless sorrows on earth, beyond the reach of all human alleviation.

The sympathy of Jesus is alone exalted—pure—infinite—removed from all taint of selfishness. He has Himself passed through every experience of woe. There are no depths of sorrow or anguish into which I can be plunged but His everlasting arms are lower still. He has been called "The great sympathetic nerve of His Church, over which the afflictions, and oppressions, and sufferings of His people continually pass." Child of sorrow, a human heart beats on the throne, and He has your name written on that heart. He cares for you as if none other claimed His regard. As the Great High Priest, He walks in the midst of his temple lamps, His golden candlesticks, replenishing them, at times, with oil—trimming them, if need be, at other times—but all in order that they may burn with a steadier and purer luster.

"He was *in all points* tempted" (Heb. 4:15). Blessed assurance! I never can know the sorrow into which the Man of Sorrows cannot enter; ah, rather, in the midst of earth's most lacerating trials, let me listen to the unanswerable challenge from the lips of a suffering Savior, "Was there ever 'any sorrow like unto my sorrow'" (Lam. 1:12)? Yet He refused not to drink the cup of wrath! He shrunk not back from the appointed cross! "He steadfastly set His face to go to Jerusalem" (Luke 9:51). And even when He hung upon the bitter tree, He refused the vinegar that would have assuaged the rage of thirst and mitigated physical suffering.

Are we tempted at times to murmur under God's afflicting hand? "Consider Him that endured . . . lest you be weary and faint in your minds" (Heb. 12:3). Shall we hesitate to bear any trial our Lord and Master sees necessary to lay upon us, when we think of the infinitely weightier Cross He so meekly and uncomplainingly carried for us?

Afflicted one, have your eye on this radiant Bow in your Cloud of

Sorrow—you may, like the disciples on the Transfiguration Mount fear to enter the cloud, but hear the voice issuing from it, "This is my Beloved Son: hear *Him*." (Mark 9:7).

Jesus speaks through these clouds! He tells us our cares are His cares, our sorrows His sorrows. He has some wise and gracious end in every mysterious chastisement. His language is, "hear the rod and who has appointed it" (Micah 6:9). He has too kind and loving a heart to cause us one needless or superfluous pang.

Oh, that we may indeed hear the voice out of the cloud, and seek that the trials He sends in love may be greatly sanctified. Let us not dream that affliction of itself is a pathway to Heaven. Clouds do not form the material rainbow. These glorious hues come from the sun-beams alone. Without the latter, who could discern nothing but blackened heavens and dismal rain torrents.

It is not because those clad in "white robes" had "come out of great tribulation" that they were enjoying the beautiful Presence; but because they had "washed their robes, and made them white in the blood of the Lamb" (Rev. 7:14). We have only reason to glory in affliction when it has been the means of bringing us nearer the Savior, and leading us to the opened Fountain.

> "And it shall come to pass,
> when I bring a cloud over the earth,
> that the bow shall be seen in the cloud."

Jesus! my only hope thou art,
Strength of my failing flesh and heart;

Oh! could I catch a smile from thee,
And drop into Eternity!

(Dictated by Charles Wesley on his death bed, 1707-1788)

- *Day 30* -

A Speedy Coming

"For yet a little while, and he that shall come
will come and will not tarry."
Hebrews 10:37

"A *little* while," and the unquiet dream of life will be over, and the "morning *without clouds*" (2 Sam. 23:4) shall dawn. A few more tossings on life's tempestuous sea, and the peaceful haven shall be entered. A few more night-watches, and the Lord of love will be seen standing on the heavenly shore, as once He did on the shores of an earthly lake, with an eternal banquet of love prepared for His *Children.*

Yes, "He cometh"—that is the Church's "blessed hope" (Titus 2:13)! It is the voice and presence of her Beloved which will "turn the shadow of death into the morning" (Amos 5:8). The dead—the ransomed dead—shall "hear His voice and come forth"—those "asleep in Jesus" God is to bring "with Him" (see John 11:43; 1 Thess. 4:13-14). His final invitation is not, "Go, you blessed, to some bright paradise of angels prepared elsewhere for you," but, "Come, share My bliss, be partakers in my crown," enter into the joy of Your Lord!" (Matt. 25:23). Paul's Heaven was described in two words, "*with* Christ" (Phil. 1:23). John's Heaven is made up of the two elements—of likeness *to* Jesus, and fellowship *with* Jesus: "we shall be like Him," and "we shall see Him as He is." (1 John 3:2). In his sublime apocalyptic visions, when "the door was opened in Heaven," the first object which attracts his arrested gaze is "One who sat upon the throne," around whom was "a rainbow in appearance like an emerald" (Rev 4:1-3).

Our happiness will not be complete until we are ushered into the full vision and fruition of Jesus. We are nourished in this far-off land from the King's country; but we shall not be satisfied until we see the King Himself. Jacob received full wagonloads from Joseph, but he could not rest till he had seen him with his own eyes. When he did so, the aged man's spirit "revived" (Gen. 45:27). We receive manifold pledges of covenant mercy from the true Joseph, in this the house of our pilgrimage, but we long to behold his face in righteousness. We shall only be "satisfied" when we "awake in His likeness" (Ps. 17:15).

"Come! Lord Jesus, come quickly" (Rev. 2:20)! "He will not tarry!" Each sun, as it sets, is bringing us nearer the joyful consummation. Time is hastening with gigantic footsteps, to the advent-throne. The sackcloth attire of a now burdened creation will soon be exchanged for the full robe of light and beauty which is to deck a Sabbath-World.

Happy day, when "the Bow," in a nobler sense, "shall be seen in the cloud"—not the Bow of Promise, but He in whom all the promises blend and center—"Behold, He comes with the clouds" (Rev. 1:7)!

Seek ever to be in an attitude of watchfulness. Like the mother of Sisera, let faith be straining its ear for the murmur of the chariot wheels (see Judg. 5:28), that when the cry shall be heard, "Behold, it is He!" we may be able joyfully to respond, "Lo! this is our God, we have waited for Him" (Isa. 25:9)!

"Blessed are those servants, whom the Lord when He comes shall find watching: verily I say unto you that He shall gird Himself, and make them to sit down to meat, and will come forth and serve them" (Luke 12:37).

> "And it shall come to pass,
> when I bring a cloud over the earth,
> that the bow shall be seen in the cloud."

> *There is a balm for every pain,*
> *A medicine for all sorrow;*
> *The eye turned backward to the Cross,*
> *And forward to the morrow.*

(Taken from *The Hope of His Coming* by Gerhard Tersteegen, 1697-1769)

- *Day 31* -

Eternal Joy

"And the ransomed of the Lord shall return, and
come to Zion with songs, and everlasting joy upon
their heads: they shall obtain joy and gladness,
and sorrow and sighing shall flee away."
Isaiah 35:10

Believer, I leave your "Bow in the cloud" behind you; and with your eye on the "Rainbow round about the throne" (Rev. 4:8), think of the glad return of God's ransomed ones to Zion—every teardrop dried, every pang forgotten!

Once wanderers "in the wilderness, in a solitary way"; prisoners "bound with affliction and iron"; mariners "staggering" in a tempest (Ps. 107:4, 10, 27)—mark the termination of their checkered history. God is not only represented as comforting their fainting souls, smashing in pieces their chains, and enabling them to batter the angry surges; but He leads the pilgrims to "a city of habitation" (Ps. 107:7); He rescues the captives from "darkness and the shadow of death" (Ps. 107:14). He brings the storm-tossed seamen to their "desired haven" (Ps. 107:30), and puts the everlasting song into the lips of all, "Oh that men would praise the LORD for his goodness, and for his wonderful works to the children of men" (Ps. 107:31).

Sorrowing one, tossed on life's stormy sea, soon will that peaceful Haven be yours. From the sunlit shores of glory, each and all of your trials will be seen to be special proofs of your heavenly Father's faithfulness—encircled with a halo of love! You may now be going forth weeping, "bearing precious seed, but you shall doubtless come again with rejoicing, bringing your sheaves with you" (Ps. 126:6).

As some seeds require on earth to be steeped in water before they germinate, so is immortal seed often here steeped in tears. But "they that sow in tears shall reap in *joy*" (Ps. 126:5). Though "weeping" may endure for the night, joy comes in the morning (Ps. 30:5)! "You are," says Samuel Rutherford (1600-1661), "upon the entry of Heaven's harvest; the losses that I write of are but summer showers, and the Sun of the new Jerusalem shall quickly dry them up." The "song of the night" shall then blend with the song of the skies, and inner, glorious meanings will be disclosed to sight, which are now hidden from the eye of faith!

"Sorrow and sighing shall forever flee away" (Isa. 35:10)!

"No sickness, no sorrow, no pain," said an aged saint now entered on these glorious realities; "but this is only Your negative. What, O God! must be Your positive?" "Songs," "everlasting joy," "joy and gladness," it will be song upon song, joy upon joy, gladness upon gladness! These songs of Heaven will be *songs of degrees*. The ransomed will be ever graduating in bliss, mounting *from glory to glo-*

ry, each song suggesting the keynote of a louder and loftier tune.

Reader, are you mourning the loss of those who *are not*; the music of whose voices is hushed for the *forever of time*, and who have left you to travel companionless and alone the wilderness journey? A few more fears, a few more tears, and you shall meet them in the daybreak of glory! Nay, more—they have but anticipated you in an earlier crown. If they have left you behind for a little season to continue your night-song, think with bounding heart of that eternal day, when, looking back on the clouds floating in the far distance in the nether Valley, you shall be able to join in the anthem said to be sung by the four-and-twenty elders as they gaze on the throne encircled by the "Rainbow of emerald," for "they rest not day and night, saying, 'Holy, holy, holy. Lord God Almighty'" (Rev. 4:3, 8).

Lord of our souls! Thou Savior ever dear,
Be still our Rainbow in the clouds of life;
In Thy pure sunlight melt each rising tear—
Our Arc of Triumph in the scenes of strife.

Radiant with mercy, calm the sinking heart,
And beam through sorrow's night and suff'ring's gloom,
A deathless Iris that will not depart,
But shine with hues unfading o'er the tomb!

"And it shall come to pass,
when I bring a cloud over the earth,
that the Bow shall be seen in the cloud."

More books by Ralph I. Tilley

Thirsting for God

Letters from Noah
(historical fiction)

The Mind of Christ
by John R. MacDuff
Introduction by Ralph I. Tilley
(edited reprint)

A Passion for Christ

How Christ Came to Church:
An Anthology of the Works of A. J. Gordon
Introduction by Ralph I. Tilley
(edited reprint)

Breath of God

The Christian's Vital Breath

Not Peace But a Sword
by Vance Havner
Introduction by Ralph I. Tilley
(fiction reprint)

Christ in You

The Bow in the Cloud
by John R. MacDuff
Introduction by Ralph I. Tilley
(edited reprint)

books available at . . .

litsjournal.org
amazon.com

Made in the USA
Middletown, DE
23 February 2021

34270026R00066